Federal Continuity Directive 2 (FCD 2)

Federal Executive Branch Mission Essential Function and Primary Mission Essential Function Identification and Submission Process

February 2008

Homeland
Security

Homeland Security

In May 2007, the National Security Presidential Directive-51/Homeland Security Presidential Directive-20 (NSPD-51/HSPD-20) *National Continuity Policy* was issued by the President to provide an updated, integrated approach to maintain a national continuity capability in order to ensure the preservation of our form of Government under the Constitution and the continuing performance of National Essential Functions under all conditions. In August 2007, the *National Continuity Policy Implementation Plan* was issued by the Assistant to the President for Homeland Security to build upon the *Policy* and provide guidance to executive branch departments and agencies in identifying and carrying out their Primary Mission Essential Functions that support the eight National Essential Functions—the most critical functions necessary to lead and sustain the nation during a catastrophic emergency.

To provide additional operational guidance to implement this policy and assist the departments and agencies in identifying their Mission Essential Functions and potential Primary Mission Essential Functions, the Department of Homeland Security developed and issues *Federal Continuity Directive 2.* This document provides guidance and direction for the departments and agencies in the process for identification of their essential functions, and the Business Process Analysis and Business Impact Analysis that support and identify the relationships between these essential functions.

The provisions of *Federal Continuity Directive 2* are applicable to all levels of Federal executive branch organizations regardless of their location, and are also useful for State, local, territorial, and tribal governments and the private sector.

Michael Chertoff
Secretary
Department of Homeland Security

TABLE OF CONTENTS

FEDERAL CONTINUITY DIRECTIVE 2 (FCD 2)

Number	Date	Office
FCD 2	February 2008	FEMA National Continuity Programs

TO: HEADS OF FEDERAL DEPARTMENTS AND AGENCIES

SUBJECT: FEDERAL EXECUTIVE BRANCH MISSION ESSENTIAL FUNCTION AND PRIMARY MISSION ESSENTIAL FUNCTION IDENTIFICATION AND SUBMISSION PROCESS

1. **PURPOSE:** This Federal Continuity Directive (FCD) implements the requirements of Federal Continuity Directive 1, ANNEX C. It provides guidance and direction to Federal executive branch departments and agencies for identification of their Mission Essential Functions (MEFs) and potential Primary Mission Essential Functions (PMEFs). It includes guidance and checklists to assist departments and agencies in assessing their essential functions through a risk management process and in identifying potential PMEFs that support the National Essential Functions (NEFs) – the most critical functions necessary to lead and sustain the nation during a catastrophic emergency. The FCD provides direction on the formalized process for submission of a department's or agency's potential PMEFs that are supportive of the NEFs. It also includes guidance on the processes for conducting a Business Process Analysis (BPA) and Business Impact Analysis (BIA) for each of the potential PMEFs that assist in identifying essential function relationships and interdependencies, time sensitivities, threat and vulnerability analyses, and mitigation strategies that impact and support the PMEFs.

2. **APPLICABILITY AND SCOPE:** The provisions of this FCD are applicable to the executive departments enumerated in 5 U.S.C. § 101, including the Department of Homeland Security, independent establishments as defined by 5 U.S.C. § 104(1), Government corporations as defined by 5 U.S.C. § 103(1), and the United States Postal Service. The departments, agencies, and independent organizations are hereinafter referred to as "agencies."

3. **AUTHORITIES:**

   See ANNEX C – Authorities and References

4. **REFERENCES:**

   See ANNEX C – Authorities and References

5. **POLICY:** It is the policy of the United States to maintain a comprehensive and effective continuity capability composed of Continuity of Operations (COOP) and Continuity of

Government (COG) programs to ensure the preservation of our form of government under the Constitution and the continuing performance of the National Essential Functions under all conditions. The ultimate goal of continuity in the executive branch is the continuation of National Essential Functions (NEFs). In order to achieve that goal, the objective for executive departments and agencies is to identify their Mission Essential Functions (MEFs) and the Primary Mission Essential Functions (PMEFs) that support the NEFs and ensure that those functions can be continued through-out, or resumed rapidly after, a disruption of normal activities. While the Federal government provides myriad services to the American people, it is important to identify those services that must be continued during an emergency. Setting priorities is difficult, but organizations should not wait for a crisis to determine what is important. The continuous performance of essential functions must be guaranteed with the right people, the right resources, and the right planning. Continuity cannot be an afterthought for organizations as they strive to perform their essential functions. In support of this policy, the Federal executive branch has developed and implemented a continuity of operations program which is composed of efforts within individual agencies to ensure that their MEFs and PMEFs continue to be performed during a wide range of emergencies including localized acts of nature, accidents, and technological or attack-related emergencies. All agencies, regardless of their size or location, shall have in place a viable continuity capability to ensure continued performance of those agencies' essential functions under all conditions.

6. **MEF AND POTENTIAL PMEF IDENTIFICATION**: The National Continuity Policy Implementation Plan provides a formalized process that enables agencies to identify their PMEFs and ensure that they are in support of the NEFs. This process is further outlined in FCD 1, *Federal Executive Branch National Continuity Program*, as part of the elements of a viable continuity capability. Annex A to this FCD provides the detailed process for identifying MEFs and potential PMEFs. It also includes guidance for conducting a BPA and BIA for the potential PMEFs.

7. **SUBMISSION REQUIREMENTS:**

   a. **MEF and Potential PMEF Identification Process:** Agencies will follow the process outlined in Annex A to identify their MEFs and potential PMEFs. Agencies will also conduct a BPA for each of their MEFs to identify the inputs, outputs, resources, systems, facilities, expertise, authorities, and internal and external interdependencies that impact their ability to conduct and support the MEFs and potential PMEFs.

   b. **Submission Timeline:** As mandated by the National Continuity Policy Implementation Plan, potential department and agency PMEFs and supporting materials must be submitted to the Department of Homeland Security (DHS) within 90 days of approval of FCD 2.

   c. **Submission Materials:** The following materials should be submitted as part of an agency's Potential PMEF Submission Package:

      1. Agency Memorandum. A memorandum from the agency head, confirming the validation of the agency's MEFs and identifying the potential PMEFs for submission and review by the Interagency Board (IAB). The IAB is chaired by the Assistant to the President for Homeland Security, and described in the National Continuity Policy Implementation Plan. This memorandum should also include the contact information (name, email address, and phone number) for the agency's Continuity Coordinator, as

described in NSPD 51/HSPD 20, and supporting Continuity Manager for potential follow-up coordination.

2. MEF/PMEF Workbook. The MEF/PMEF Workbook consists of a series of worksheets that are provided in MS Excel format or other compatible format. These worksheets, located in Attachment A, identify requirements, inputs, outputs, interdependencies and other critical elements that assist departments and agencies in identifying their MEFs and potential PMEFs and in completing the required BPAs. The PMEF BIA Worksheet is not required to be submitted to DHS for IAB review until after the National Continuity Coordinator (NCC) has approved the department or agency PMEFs (and is not required as part of the 90 day submission process). **Since each of the department and agency approved PMEFs and supporting worksheets will be loaded into the Readiness Reporting System (RRS) for processing, it is critical that the format of the spreadsheets not be modified.**

3. Candidate PMEF Narrative Sheet. The Candidate PMEF Narrative Sheet is an MS Word document or other compatible format. Its purpose is to provide a narrative summary of candidate PMEFs to compliment the MEF/PMEF Workbook material. Each Candidate PMEF Narrative Sheet will include organization and point of contact; PMEF statement; PMEF description; impact if the specific PMEF is not conducted; supporting MEF(s) linked to the PMEF; supported NEFs; maximum tolerable downtime; and the names of interdependent partners.

4. A checklist for agency submissions is located at Attachment E.

d. **Submission Process:** In accordance with guidance in the National Continuity Policy Implementation Plan, departments and agencies should submit both a paper and electronic copy on CD of their Potential PMEF Submission Package to:

> U.S. Department of Homeland Security
> Federal Emergency Management Agency (FEMA)
> National Continuity Programs Directorate
> 500 C Street, SW, Room 524
> Washington, D.C. 20472

The Agency Memorandum should be submitted using a portable document format (pdf) file. The MEF/PMEF Workbook information will be submitted in the electronic spreadsheet format provided to facilitate the transfer of the information into RRS. Questions or comments related to department or agency submissions should be submitted to FEMA's National Continuity Programs Directorate, (202) 646-4145 or email at FEMA-pmefsubmissions@dhs.gov.

Only unclassified information should be submitted to the FEMA-pmefsubmissions@dhs.gov email account. Agencies that need to submit classified material should contact FEMA Document Control at (202) 646-4629.

e. **Scope of Responses:** An agency's submission should include an analysis of all their government functions, at all locations, and should not be limited to Headquarters activities.

8. **ADDITIONAL GUIDANCE:** In addition to the information provided in this FCD, familiarization briefings and training on the MEF and potential PMEF identification process

will be provided for agency Continuity Coordinators and Managers. These briefings and training will be conducted within 60 days following the publication of the National Continuity Policy Implementation Plan and updated annually along with other continuity training courses. Attachment B contains the presentation slides for the Assistant Secretary/Continuity Coordinator familiarization briefing, and Attachment C contains the Continuity Manager/Planner training briefing. The dates, times, locations, and other logistics for these briefings will be provided via separate correspondence.

9. **POINT OF CONTACT:** Should you have any questions or require assistance with the information contained in the FCD, please contact the FEMA National Continuity Programs Directorate at (202) 646-4145.

10. **DISTRIBUTION:** This FCD is distributed to the heads of Federal departments and agencies, Continuity Coordinators and Managers, senior policy officials, and other interested continuity and emergency preparedness officials.

ANNEX A. MEF & POTENTIAL PMEF IDENTIFICATION PROCESS

OVERVIEW

The Federal executive branch recognizes that the entire spectrum of government functions may not be performed or needed in the immediate aftermath of an emergency. Indeed, in a crisis, resources may be scarce. Allocating resources based on sound planning helps to ensure that the delivery of essential functions and services will remain uninterrupted across a wide range of potential emergencies and provides a mechanism for the resumption of all functions as resources become available.

An agency should carefully review all of its missions and functions before determining those that are essential. Improperly identifying or not identifying functions as "essential" can impair the effectiveness of the entire continuity program, because other aspects of the plans are designed around supporting these functions. If an agency fails to identify a function as essential, the agency will not identify the requirements and resources to support that function in an emergency and not make the necessary coordination and arrangements to perform that function. If an agency identifies too many functions as essential, the agency risks being unable to adequately address all of them. In either case, the agency increases the risk that it will not be able to perform all of its essential functions during a continuity event.

Planning related to essential functions must also include identifying those agency partners who are critical to program delivery, testing the effectiveness of data exchange among the organization's partners, developing complementary continuity plans with those partners, sharing key information on readiness with partners and the public, and taking steps to ensure that the performance of the agency's essential functions will be sustained during a continuity event. There must be careful consideration of agency and other partner interdependencies, to ensure the continued delivery and performance of essential functions across a full spectrum of threats and all-hazards emergencies.

Continuity cannot occur without the commitment and dedication of many partners who play integral roles in ensuring homeland security and providing critical functions and services to the Nation's citizens.

Figure 1

These partners include the following (see Figure 1):

- Federal Government: legislative branch, executive branch (including all agencies), and judicial branch;
- State, local, territorial, and tribal governments; and
- Private sector critical infrastructure owners and operators.

ESSENTIAL FUNCTIONS:

To support its continuity requirements, the Federal executive branch recognizes the following three categories of essential functions:

- Mission Essential Functions (MEFs): The limited set of department and agency-level government functions that must be continued after a disruption of normal activities.

- Primary Mission Essential Functions (PMEFs): A subset of agency MEFs that directly support the NEFs.

- National Essential Functions (NEFs): The eight functions the President and national leadership will focus on to lead and sustain the nation during a catastrophic emergency.

To support the Nation's continuity preparedness, all agencies must identify and prioritize their essential functions as the foundation for continuity planning. Essential functions, broadly speaking, are those functions that enable an organization to provide vital services, exercise civil authority, maintain the safety of the general public, and sustain the industrial/economic base during an emergency.

IDENTIFICATION OF MEFS AND POTENTIAL PMEFS:

Federal agencies will use the following two-step process to assist in identifying MEFs and the potential PMEFs that support the NEFs.

Step 1: Process for MEF Identification (see Figure 2)

Agencies will conduct the following steps when identifying and analyzing MEFs:
- Reviewing their organization's functions as directed by applicable law, presidential directives, executive orders, or other executive branch directives, to identify their MEFs.
- Conducting a MEF BPA to identify and map the functional processes, workflows, activities, personnel expertise, systems, data, and facilities inherent to the execution of each identified MEF (e.g., define how each MEF is performed and executed, using a business process flow map) that must be performed under all circumstances either uninterrupted, with minimal interruption, or requiring immediate execution in an emergency.
- Identifying those MEFs that provide vital interdependent support to a MEF performed by another agency or by an Emergency Support Function (ESF) under the National Response Framework (NRF).
- Identifying those MEFs that require vital support from another agency to ensure the execution of their mission and identify when and where the particular interdependency is executed within the BPA business process flow.
- Validating and approving the identified MEFs and BPA by each agency head.

Step 2: Process for PMEF Identification

This process is divided into two sections: the first is completed by agencies and the second is completed by the IAB.

PMEF identification is an iterative process performed by each department and agency in coordination with the NCC. In order to identify and analyze PMEFs, upon MEF approval by each department or agency head, a joint effort between the NCC and each department or agency Continuity Coordinator and staff will result in a preliminary identification of PMEFs that potentially support NEFs. The joint effort will culminate in the department's or agency's submission of PMEF identification results to the NCC for further interagency analysis.

An IAB, established by the NCC, conducts a review of submitted potential PMEFs and validates their relationship to the NEFs. A risk management methodology (i.e., BPA or BIA) will be used to ensure that the PMEFs are appropriate and relevant. (See Appendix 1 to Annex A) Once the IAB and the department or agency has completed a joint review and validation of the potential

PMEFs and the NCC has approved the PMEFs, a BIA will be conducted by the department or agency.

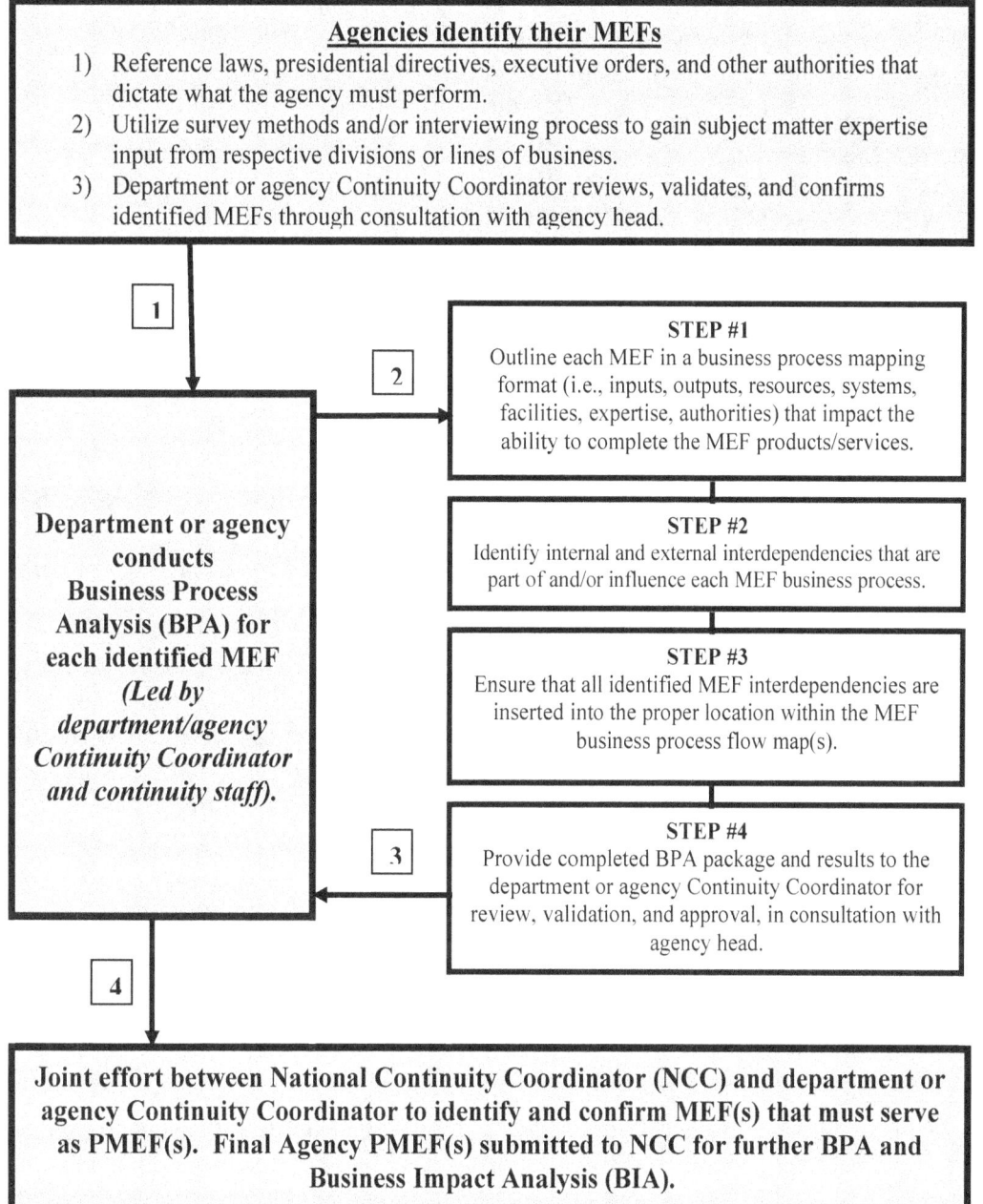

Agencies identify their MEFs
1) Reference laws, presidential directives, executive orders, and other authorities that dictate what the agency must perform.
2) Utilize survey methods and/or interviewing process to gain subject matter expertise input from respective divisions or lines of business.
3) Department or agency Continuity Coordinator reviews, validates, and confirms identified MEFs through consultation with agency head.

Department or agency conducts Business Process Analysis (BPA) for each identified MEF *(Led by department/agency Continuity Coordinator and continuity staff).*

STEP #1
Outline each MEF in a business process mapping format (i.e., inputs, outputs, resources, systems, facilities, expertise, authorities) that impact the ability to complete the MEF products/services.

STEP #2
Identify internal and external interdependencies that are part of and/or influence each MEF business process.

STEP #3
Ensure that all identified MEF interdependencies are inserted into the proper location within the MEF business process flow map(s).

STEP #4
Provide completed BPA package and results to the department or agency Continuity Coordinator for review, validation, and approval, in consultation with agency head.

Joint effort between National Continuity Coordinator (NCC) and department or agency Continuity Coordinator to identify and confirm MEF(s) that must serve as PMEF(s). Final Agency PMEF(s) submitted to NCC for further BPA and Business Impact Analysis (BIA).

Figure 2: Process for MEF Identification

MEF AND POTENTIAL PMEF WORKSHEETS

To assist in the MEF and potential PMEF identification process, this Annex provides guidance for identifying MEFs and potential PMEFs as well as for conducting a BPA and BIA for potential PMEFs. To assist agencies in implementing and documenting this process, Attachment A contains multiple worksheets that comprise the Potential PMEF Submission Package Workbook. The worksheets found in the MS Excel workbook are as follows:

a) **Organizational Information Worksheet**
b) **MEF Identification Worksheet 1**
c) **MEF Identification Worksheet 2**
d) **MEF Business Process Analysis (BPA) Worksheet**
e) **MEF Business Process Elements Worksheet**
f) **Potential PMEF Screening Worksheet**
g) **PMEF Candidate Worksheet**
h) **PMEF Business Impact Analysis (BIA) Worksheet** (to be completed after NCC approval of PMEFs)
i) **Supporting Remarks Worksheet** (as necessary)
j) **NEF Reference List**
k) **Definitions**
l) **Impact Values and Hazard List**

By completing worksheets "a" through "g", a department or agency will identify their potential PMEFs and complete the required BPAs.

GOVERNMENT FUNCTIONS AND MISSION ESSENTIAL FUNCTIONS

Agencies at every level of government provide a broad cross-section of government functions. The task of separating MEFs from those government functions is an early and critical component of continuity planning. Preparing a list of all the government functions performed by an agency is a prerequisite to identifying those specific actions which must be performed in order to implement one or more essential functions.

The identification of government functions will focus on defining the activities that are conducted to accomplish the agency's mission and serve its stakeholders. The proper identification of government functions and MEFs will be beneficial in implementing continuity programs and reconstitution plans before and after an event. The relationship between government functions and MEFs is outlined in Figures 3 and 4.

Government Functions (see Figure 3) are the collective functions of agencies, as defined by the Constitution, statute, regulation, presidential direction or other legal authorities, and the functions of the legislative and judicial branches. The activities of State, local, territorial, tribal governments and private sector organizations often support Federal government functions, particularly in the protection of critical infrastructure and key resources (CI/KR). These interdependencies rely upon a greater interoperability between and among these partners, to facilitate a more rapid and effective response to and recovery from any emergency.

Figure 3

Figure 4

MEFs are described as the limited set of agency-level government functions (see Figure 4) that must be continued throughout, or resumed rapidly after, a disruption of normal activities. MEFs are those functions that enable an organization to provide vital services, exercise civil authority, maintain the safety of the public, and sustain the industrial and economic base, during the disruption of normal operations. Once identified, MEFs serve as key continuity planning factors for agencies to determine appropriate staffing, communications, information, facilities, training, and other continuity requirements.

Mission Essential Function (MEF) Identification

For a government function to be identified as a MEF, the National Continuity Policy Implementation Plan provides a screening aide (see Figure 5).

MEF Initial Screening Aid		
Is the function directed by law, presidential directive, or executive order? If yes, identify which:	YES	NO
Did a BPA determine that the function must be performed under all circumstances either uninterrupted, with minimal interruption, or requiring immediate execution in an emergency?	YES	NO
If the answer to one or both of these questions is "No," the function is probably not a MEF.		

Figure 5: MEF Initial Screening Aid

The MEF Identification Worksheets will assist agencies in applying these identified tests.

MEF Identification Worksheets

Before a government function can be considered a MEF, it must first meet the legal test as outlined in the National Continuity Policy Implementation Plan. MEF Identification Worksheet 1 (see Figure 6) screens each identified government function to confirm it is legally directed and therefore should be considered a potential MEF. This worksheet also addresses interdependency requirements and identifies partners required for each function by department and agency name.

Table 1 provides the component details for the MEF Identification Worksheet 1. Each column entry is described in greater detail to assist in completing the worksheet. All components included on the worksheet need to be considered and each column filled out, as appropriate, in order to determine if this function will continue to be considered for the next step of the process. If the legal test is met, then that function will be further reviewed using MEF Identification Worksheet 2. Interdependencies will be identified and linked to the function and used throughout the process.

Figure 6: MEF Identification Worksheet 1

Table 1: MEF Identification Worksheet 1 Column Descriptions

WORKSHEET COLUMN	DESCRIPTION
Entry #	Enter the sequential number of the identified government function. Note: This entry number does not change from sheet to sheet and is the primary identifier of each line item that is transferred between sheets.
Dept/Agency	Enter department or agency identification
Sub-element or Department component	Identify component or sub-element, if applicable
Government Functions	Identify the government function. Do not include enabling or supporting tasks. Do not include capability requirements.
Constitution	Place the letter 'X' in the cell if this authority applies.
Regulation	Place the letter 'X' in the cell if this authority applies.
Presidential Directive	Place the letter 'X' in the cell if this authority applies.
Executive Order	Place the letter 'X' in the cell if this authority applies.
Court Ruling or Decision	Place the letter 'X' in the cell if this authority applies.
Other Legal Authority	Place the letter 'X' in the cell if other not previously identified mandated legal authority applies.
Meets Legal Test (Y/N)	If one of the legal test cells is marked with an 'X' then the function meets the legal test and is identified with a 'Y' for yes. Otherwise, insert the letter 'N' for no. **If the answer is no, then this function will probably not meet the test to be a MEF.**
Requires International Partner	Identify any interdependency at the appropriate level(s). There can be more than one cell selected as an interdependency. Place the letter 'X' in the cell.
Requires Federal Partner Support	Identify any interdependency at the appropriate level(s). There can be more than one cell selected as an interdependency. Place the letter 'X' in the cell.
Requires State Partner Support	Identify any interdependency at the appropriate level(s). There can be more than one cell selected as an interdependency. Place the letter 'X' in the cell.
Requires Local Partner Support	Identify any interdependency at the appropriate level(s). There can be more than one cell selected as an interdependency. Place the letter 'X' in the cell.
Requires Territorial Partner Support	Identify any interdependency at the appropriate level(s). There can be more than one cell selected as an interdependency. Place the letter 'X' in the cell.
Requires Tribal Partner Support	Identify any interdependency at the appropriate level(s). There can be more than one cell selected as an interdependency. Place the letter 'X' in the cell.
Requires Private Sector Partner Support	Identify any interdependency at the appropriate level(s). There can be more than one cell selected as an interdependency. Place the letter 'X' in the cell.
Interdependency Identified (Y/N)	If any of the interdependency test cells are identified then 'Y' for yes. Otherwise insert the letter 'N' for no.

WORKSHEET COLUMN	DESCRIPTION
List internal and external partners required to perform function	For each 'X' identified in the interdependency test, list by name the organization(s), to include the component and subcomponent where possible, required to perform this government function.

MEF Identification Worksheet 2 (see Figure 7) documents the second step in identifying whether a government function is a candidate to become a MEF. The purpose of this step and accompanying worksheet is to analyze whether the function must be performed under all circumstances either uninterrupted, with minimal interruption, or will require immediate execution in an emergency. This worksheet also addresses specific time sensitivity considerations that are essential in determining if the government function must be performed during a crisis/hazard situation and incorporated into continuity planning. Upon completion of this worksheet, agencies will have identified the information required to establish their MEFs and will then begin the BPA for each MEF to further assist in identifying potential PMEFs.

Figure 7: MEF Identification Worksheet 2

Table 2 shows the component details for MEF Identification Worksheet 2. Each column in the worksheet is further described in greater detail to assist in completing the worksheet. Upon completion of MEF Identification Worksheet 2, the department or agency Continuity Coordinator should review and validate the completed MEF Identification Worksheets in the final column of MEF Identification Worksheet 2.

Table 2: MEF Identification Worksheet 2 Column Descriptions

WORKSHEET COLUMN	DESCRIPTION
Entry #	Enter the sequential number of the identified government function.
Dept/Agency	Enter the department or agency's name.
Sub-element or Department component	Identify subordinate element, if applicable.
Government Functions	Identify the government function. Does not include enabling or supporting tasks. Does not include capability requirements.

WORSHEET COLUMN	DESCRIPTION
List products or operations impacted if function is not performed	Identify all products/outputs that result from the performance of the government function.
Perform w/o interruption	Place the letter 'X' in the cell if the level of criticality for the government function in a crisis/hazard situation or emergency requires performance without interruption.
Minimal Interruption	Place the letter 'X' in the cell if the level of criticality for the government function in a crisis/hazard situation or emergency requires performance with minimal interruption.
Immediately execute in emergency	Place the letter 'X' in the cell if the level of criticality for the government function in a crisis/hazard situation or emergency requires immediate execution.
Support to another D/A MEF/PMEF	Place the letter 'X' in the appropriate cell if performance of the government function supports the performance of MEF/PMEF of another department or agency.
Supports ESF for NRF	Place the letter 'X' in the appropriate cell if performance of the government function supports the performance of an ESF for the NRF.
Assess Impact if not performed	Determine the level of criticality for a government function in a crisis/hazard situation or emergency. Consider the criticality of the outputs/products that would result from the completion of the function. Criticality is assessed on a scale from 1-10.

• **10-Critically High** Exceptionally grave impact preventing mission performance and the ability to implement corrective actions	• **6-Medium High** Moderate to serious impact requiring corrective action, where the negative effect will result in slight mission delays
• **9-Extremely High** Grave impact requiring corrective action and negative effect results in delays to mission for an extended period of time	• **5-Medium** Moderate impact requiring corrective action, where the negative effect will not impact mission completion
• **8-Very High** Serious impact requiring corrective action and negative effect results in delays to mission for a limited period of time	• **4-Medium Low** Minimal impact requiring corrective action, where negative effect will not impact mission completion
• **7-High** Serious impact requiring corrective action, where the negative effect will result in minor mission delays	• **3-Low** Minimal impact or consequence without long term negative effects
	• **2-Very Low** Negligible consequences or impact with minimal long term negative effect
	• **1-Extremely Low** Negligible consequences or impact with no long term negative effect

WORSHEET COLUMN	DESCRIPTION
0 hrs	Place an 'X' in the cell for the function if it must be performed immediately without interruption. This should be considered in conjunction with the criticality assessment (i.e., is the function required to be performed without interruption?)
< 12 hrs	Place an 'X' in the cell for the function if it must be performed with less than 12 hours of interruption. This should be considered in conjunction with the criticality assessment.
< 24 hrs	Place an 'X' in the cell for the function if it must be performed with less than 24 hours of interruption. This should be considered in conjunction with the criticality assessment.
≤ 30 days	Place an 'X' in the cell for the function if it must be performed within 30 days of interruption. This should be considered in conjunction with the criticality assessment.

WORKSHEET COLUMN	DESCRIPTION
Time Sensitive (Y/N)	If any of the time sensitivity cells are identified then 'Y' for yes. Otherwise insert the letter 'N' for no. **If the function is not time sensitive it will probably not meet the test to become a MEF.**
D/A CC Validated	The department or agency Continuity Coordinator initials that the government functions have been assessed for consideration as a MEF.

Government functions that have met the MEF legal and time sensitivity requirements should be designated by the department or agency as a MEF. Each MEF will then be transferred to the MEF BPA Worksheet to continue to guide the user through the steps of the BPA.

Mission Essential Function Business Process Analysis (BPA) Worksheet

The MEF BPA Worksheet (see Figure 8) captures information for each MEF by assisting with the following analysis steps:

1) List all inputs required to perform the function, identify key elements in the business process flow, list function outputs, and analyze interagency support requirements.
2) Identify interdependencies and identify those that should be contacted to determine their relationship in supporting the function, both for inputs and outputs.
3) The department or agency Continuity Coordinator reviews the MEF BPA Worksheet for approval and validation.

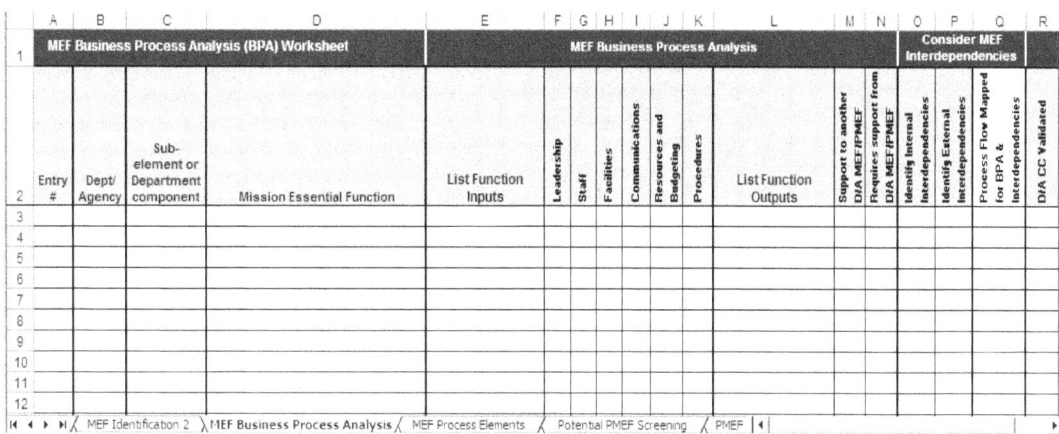

Figure 8: MEF BPA Worksheet

Table 3 shows the component details for the MEF BPA Worksheet. Each column in the worksheet is described below to assist the user in completing the worksheet.

Table 3: MEF BPA Worksheet Column Descriptions

WORKSHEET COLUMN	DESCRIPTION
Entry #	Enter the sequential number of the identified Mission Essential Function
Dept/Agency	Enter department or agency identification
Sub-element or Department component	Identify subordinate element, if applicable
Mission Essential Function	Identify the MEF candidate. This column should include those functions that met the MEF screening requirements from worksheets 1 and 2. Does not include enabling or supporting tasks. Does not include capability requirements.

WORKSHEET COLUMN	DESCRIPTION
List Function Inputs	Identify all products/inputs that are required to support the execution of this function.
Leadership	If there is a Leadership component to support this function, place the letter 'X' in the appropriate cell. Leadership includes the senior decision-makers designated to head an organization or their designated successors. Specific elements will be identified in the MEF Business Process Elements Worksheet (Figure 10).
Staff	If there is a Staff component to support this function, place the letter 'X' in the appropriate cell. Staff will include those personnel, both senior and core personnel, that provide the leadership advice, recommendations, and the functional support necessary to continue essential operations. Specific elements will be identified in the MEF Business Process Elements Worksheet (Figure 10).
Communications	If there is a Communications and/or IT system element, e.g. fixed satellite, high frequency radio, secure cellular telephone, etc., to support this function, place the letter 'X' in the appropriate cell. Communications will include voice, video, and data capabilities that enable the leadership and staff to conduct the mission essential functions of the organization. These communications must provide the ability for governments and the private sector to communicate internally and with other entities (including with other Federal agencies, State, local, territorial, and tribal governments, and the private sector), to include transition to alternate sites as necessary to perform their MEFs. Specific elements will be identified in the MEF Business Process Elements Worksheet (Figure 10).
Facilities	If there is a Facilities component to support this function, place the letter 'X' in the appropriate cell. Facilities include all locations where leadership and staffs may operate in support of essential functions during a continuity event. These include existing alternate facilities; alternate usages of existing facilities; and, as appropriate, virtual office options including telework. Specific elements will be identified in the MEF Business Process Elements Worksheet (Figure 10).
Resources and Budgeting	If there is a Resources and Budgeting component to support this function, place the letter 'X' in the appropriate cell. Consideration must be made for the acquisition of the resources necessary for continuity operations on an emergency basis. Funding for continuity programs should be based on continuity requirements and prioritized appropriately within agency budget requests. Specific elements will be identified in the MEF Business Process Elements Worksheet (Figure 10).
Procedures	If there is a Procedures component to support this function, place the letter 'X' in the appropriate cell. Procedures can include: plans, standard operating and readiness procedures, reporting procedures, memoranda of agreement (MOA)/memoranda of understanding (MOU), etc. Specific elements will be identified in the MEF Business Process Elements Worksheet (Figure 10).
List Function Outputs	Identify all products/outputs that result from the performance of the MEF. Agencies will also identify, as appropriate, the ESF number that the MEF supports.
Support to another D/A MEF/PMEF	Determine the business flow requirements as related to other department or agency MEF/PMEFs. (During the process mapping, planners contact the business POC for coordination.) Place the letter 'X' in the appropriate cell.
Requires support from a D/A MEF/PMEF	Determine the business flow requirements that are required from other department or agency MEF/PMEFs. (During the process mapping, planners contact the business POC for coordination.) Place the letter 'X' in the appropriate cell.
Identify Internal Interdependencies	Identify all internal interdependent organizations in the process flow mapping. Department or agency Continuity Coordinator can reference MEF Identification Worksheet 1 for validation.
Identify External Interdependencies	Identify all external interdependent organizations in the process flow mapping. Department or agency Continuity Coordinator can reference MEF Identification Worksheet 1 for validation.

WORKSHEET COLUMN	DESCRIPTION
Process Flow Mapped for BPA & Interdependencies	This column allows the planner to keep track of those MEFs that have been mapped for their business process flow (includes input from the MEF Business Process Elements Worksheet (Figure 10)). Upon completion of the MEF Business Process Element Worksheet for the MEF, annotate this column with an 'X'.
D/A CC Validated	The department or agency Continuity Coordinator initials that the MEF candidate has had a business process flow analysis completed and the supporting mapping has been completed.

IDENTIFICATION OF KEY ELEMENTS (INTERNAL AND EXTERNAL) FOR THE COMPONENTS OF THE BPA

After conducting the MEF BPA to identify the functional processes and requirements that include inputs and outputs and the required components that support the MEF, each MEF will require further analysis to identify key elements that support these components. This business process flow based on the components listed in the MEF BPA Worksheet is represented in Figure 9.

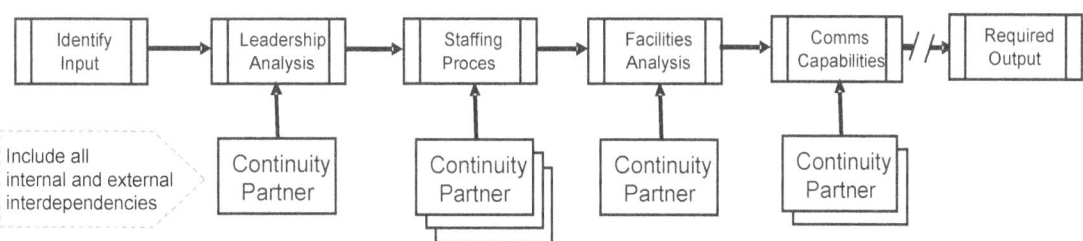

Figure 9: Requirements for MEF Business Process Flow

The MEF Business Process Elements Worksheet (see Figure 10) enables agencies to further identify key elements that support the business process flow. All identified MEF interdependencies (both internal and external) should be inserted into the proper location within the MEF business process flow. These entries should include all elements that will ensure execution of their associated MEF. Table 4 shows the component details for the MEF Business Process Elements Worksheet. Each column in the worksheet is described in the table to assist the user in completing the worksheet.

Figure 10: MEF Business Process Elements Worksheet

Table 4: MEF Business Process Elements Worksheet Column Descriptions

WORKSHEET COLUMN	DESCRIPTION
Entry #	Enter the sequential number of the identified Mission Essential Function
Dept/Agency	Enter department or agency identification
Sub-element or Department component	Identify subordinate element, if applicable
Mission Essential Function	Identify the MEF candidate. This column should include those functions that met the MEF screening requirements from MEF Identification Worksheets 1 and 2. Does not include enabling or supporting tasks. Does not include capability requirements.
Internal or External Relationship	This column allows the listing of key elements for each business process component to be separated based on whether it reflects an internal or external relationship.
Inputs	Identify all products/inputs that are required to support the execution of this function. Entries are separated to reflect whether the element is based upon an internal or external relationship.
Leadership	Identify all Leadership elements that are required to support the execution of this function. Entries are separated to reflect whether the element is based upon an internal or external relationship. Leadership includes the senior decision-makers designated to head an organization, or their designated successors. This entry is completed if Leadership was identified with an 'X' on the preceding MEF BPA Worksheet.
Staff	Identify all Staffing elements that are required to support the execution of this function. Entries are separated to reflect whether the element is based upon an internal or external relationship. Staff will include those personnel, both senior and core personnel that provide the leadership advice, recommendations, and the functional support necessary to continue essential operations. This entry is completed if Staff was identified with an 'X' on the preceding MEF BPA Worksheet.
Communications	Identify all Communication and IT system elements, e.g. fixed satellite, high frequency radio, secure cellular telephone, etc., that are required to support the execution of this function. Entries are separated to reflect whether the element is based upon an internal or external relationship. Communications will include voice, video, and data capabilities that enable the leadership and staff to conduct the mission essential functions of the organization. These communications must provide the ability for governments and the private sector to communicate internally and with other entities (including with other Federal agencies, State, local, territorial, and tribal governments, and the private sector) as necessary to perform their MEFs. This entry is completed if Communications was identified with an 'X' on the preceding MEF BPA Worksheet.
Facilities	Identify all Facilities elements that are required to support the execution of this function. Entries are separated to reflect whether the element is based upon an internal or external relationship. Facilities include all locations where leadership and staffs may operate in support of essential functions during a continuity event. These include existing alternate facilities; alternate usages of existing facilities; and, as appropriate, virtual office options including telework. This entry is completed if Facilities was identified with an 'X' on the preceding MEF BPA Worksheet.
Resources and Budgeting	Identify all Resources and Budgeting elements that are required to support the execution of this function. Entries are separated to reflect whether the element is based upon an internal or external relationship. Consideration must be made for the acquisition of the resources necessary for continuity operations on an emergency basis. Funding for continuity programs should be based on continuity requirements and prioritized appropriately within agency budget requests. This entry is completed if Resources and Budgeting was identified

WORKSHEET COLUMN	DESCRIPTION
	with an 'X' on the preceding MEF BPA Worksheet.
Procedures	Identify all Procedure elements that are required to support the execution of this function. Entries are separated to reflect whether the element is based upon an internal or external relationship. Procedures can include: plans, standard operating and readiness procedures, reporting procedures, memoranda of agreement (MOA)/memoranda of understanding (MOU), etc. This entry is completed if Procedures was identified with an 'X' on the preceding MEF BPA Worksheet.
Outputs	Identify all products/outputs that result from the performance of the MEF. Entries are separated to reflect whether the element is based upon an internal or external relationship.

Once the MEFs have been identified along with their components and supporting elements, the planning process for selecting potential PMEFs can begin.

PRIMARY MISSION ESSENTIAL FUNCTIONS

Figure 11

Figure 12

Once MEFs have been identified and analyzed using the BPA, the review process for identifying potential PMEFs can begin. Directly linking PMEFs to a NEF requires Federal executive branch agencies to identify the most critical functions that must continue during an emergency as well as the planning required to perform those functions. This model may serve as a template for other government organizations and for private sector entities.

PMEFs are those agency mission essential functions, validated by the NCC, which must be performed in order to support the performance of the NEFs before, during, and in the aftermath of an emergency (see Figure 11). PMEFs are defined as those functions that need to be continuous or resumed within 12 hours after an event and maintained for up to 30 days or until normal operations can be resumed.

In accordance with NSPD-51/HSPD-20, the eight NEFs represent the overarching responsibilities of the Federal Government to lead and sustain the Nation and shall be the primary focus of the Federal Government's leadership during and in the aftermath of an emergency (see Figure 12).

PMEF IDENTIFICATION AND ANALYSIS

The National Continuity Policy Implementation Plan provides a PMEF Initial Screening Aid to assist in identifying potential PMEFs (see Figure 13).

PMEF Initial Screening Aid		
Does the function directly support a NEF? If yes, identify which: 1 2 3 4 5 6 7 8	YES	NO
Does the function need to be continued uninterrupted or need to be resumed within 12 hours, regardless of circumstance?	YES	NO
The answers to both of these must be "YES" for the function to be considered a PMEF.		

Figure 13: Potential PMEF Initial Screening Aid

Potential PMEF Screening Worksheet

The Potential PMEF Screening Worksheet (see Figure 14) provides a screening test to identify whether a MEF is a candidate for PMEF consideration. The purpose is to analyze which NEFs are supported by each MEF and if this function must be continued within 12 hours of an interruption. Upon completion of this worksheet, agencies will have identified the information required to establish PMEF candidates. Once the IAB has reviewed the potential PMEFs with the submitting agencies and the NCC has approved the PMEFs, a BIA will be conducted by the department or agency to determine the level of risk, recovery time, criticality, and required mitigation strategies. Table 5 provides the component details for the Potential PMEF Screening Worksheet.

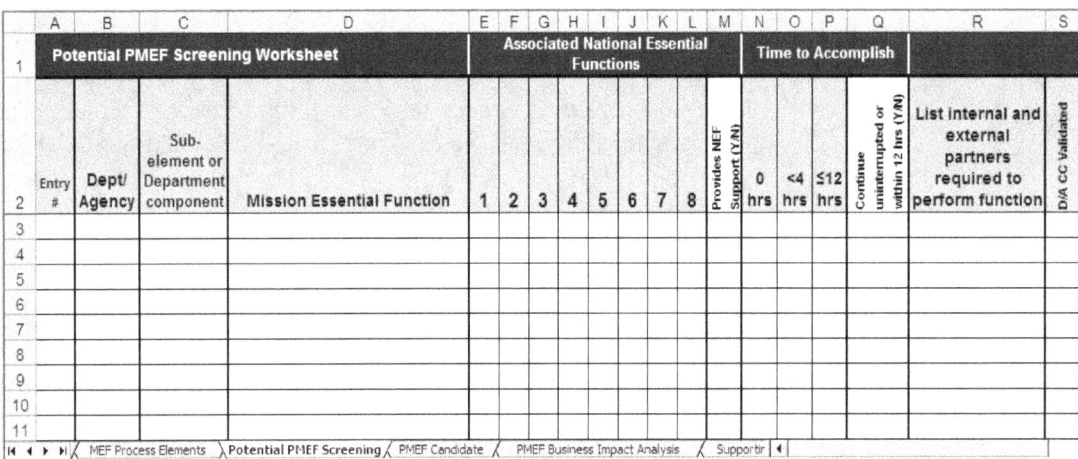

Figure 14: Potential PMEF Screening Worksheet

Table 5: Potential PMEF Screening Worksheet Column Descriptions

WORKSHEET COLUMN	DESCRIPTION
Entry #	Enter the sequential number of the identified Mission Essential Function
Dept/Agency	Enter department or agency identification
Sub-element or Department component	Identify subordinate element, if applicable
Mission Essential Function	Identify the MEF candidate. This column should include those functions that met the MEF screening requirements from MEF Identification Worksheets 1 and 2. Does not include enabling or supporting tasks. Does not include capability requirements.
NEF 1. Ensuring the continued functioning of our form of government under the Constitution, including the functioning of the three separate branches of government.	Identify whether this MEF supports this NEF. There can be more than one cell selected as supporting a NEF. Place the letter 'X' in the cell.
NEF 2. Providing leadership visible to the Nation and the world and maintaining the trust and confidence of the American people.	Identify whether this MEF supports this NEF. There can be more than one cell selected as supporting a NEF. Place the letter 'X' in the cell.
NEF 3. Defending the Constitution of the United States against all enemies, foreign and domestic, and preventing or interdicting attacks against the United States or its people, property, or interests.	Identify whether this MEF supports this NEF. There can be more than one cell selected as supporting a NEF. Place the letter 'X' in the cell.
NEF 4. Maintaining and fostering effective relationships with foreign nations.	Identify whether this MEF supports this NEF. There can be more than one cell selected as supporting a NEF. Place the letter 'X' in the cell.
NEF 5. Protecting against threats to the homeland and bringing to justice perpetrators of crimes or attacks against the United States or its people, property, or interests.	Identify whether this MEF supports this NEF. There can be more than one cell selected as supporting a NEF. Place the letter 'X' in the cell.
NEF 6. Providing rapid and effective response to and recovery from the domestic consequences of an attack or other incident.	Identify whether this MEF supports this NEF. There can be more than one cell selected as supporting a NEF. Place the letter 'X' in the cell.
NEF 7. Protecting and stabilizing the Nation's economy and ensuring public confidence in its financial systems.	Identify whether this MEF supports this NEF. There can be more than one cell selected as supporting a NEF. Place the letter 'X' in the cell.
NEF 8. Providing for critical Federal Government services that address the national health, safety, and welfare needs of the United States.	Identify whether this MEF supports this NEF. There can be more than one cell selected as supporting a NEF. Place the letter 'X' in the cell.
Provides NEF Support (Y/N)	If any of the NEFs are identified then 'Y' for yes. Otherwise insert the letter 'N' for no. **If the function does not support one or more NEFs, it will not meet the test to become a PMEF.**
0 hrs	Place an 'X' in the cell for the function if it must be performed immediately without delay.
<4 hr	Place an 'X' in the cell for the function if it must be performed with less than 4 hours of interruption (with minimal interruption).

WORKSHEET COLUMN	DESCRIPTION
≤12 hrs	Place an 'X' in the cell for the function if it must be performed with less than 12 hours of interruption.
Continue uninterrupted or within 12 hrs (Y/N)	If any of the Time to Accomplish cells are identified then 'Y' for yes. Otherwise insert the letter 'N' for no. If the function needs to be continuous or resumed within 12 hours after an event, regardless of circumstance, it will meet this test to become a PMEF.
List internal and external partners required to perform function	List, by name, the organization(s) required to perform this potential PMEF. This information should mirror what is listed in the MEF Identification Worksheets and mapped in the MEF BPA Worksheet.
D/A CC Validated	The department or agency Continuity Coordinator initials that the MEF can establish a relationship to a candidate PMEF supporting a NEF. Any PMEF candidate that is not required within 12 hours of interruption will require further explanation in the narrative submission of the process.

If the link to a NEF is established and the function needs to be continuous or resumed within 12 hours after an event, regardless of circumstances, then that function can be considered by the department or agency to the IAB as a PMEF candidate. The department or agency Continuity Coordinator must review and validate the Potential PMEF Screening Worksheet.

Potential PMEF Development / PMEF Candidate Worksheet

Upon MEF approval by each department or agency head, potential PMEFs must be developed. Each Continuity Coordinator and staff will prepare a preliminary identification of PMEFs that potentially support NEFs. To achieve this result, the department or agency must clearly and succinctly articulate a PMEF statement that embodies the specificity of the organizational mission and consists of one or more MEFs that are linked to NEF execution. The PMEF statement should identify the organizational action or role required, the conditions under which the function would be performed, the scope of operations, and standard of performance. The PMEF Candidate Worksheet (see Figure 15) is provided to capture this PMEF statement, capture which NEFs are linked from the MEF analysis on the previous worksheet, and identify the determined maximum tolerable downtime for each PMEF.

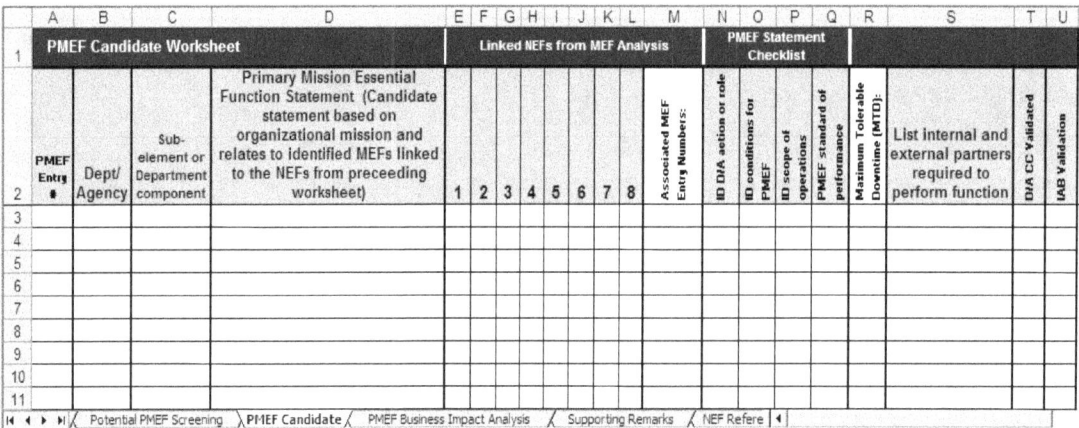

Figure 15: PMEF Candidate Worksheet

Table 6 shows the component details for the PMEF Candidate Worksheet. Each column in the worksheet is described below to assist the user in completing the worksheet. For this worksheet, a separate row should be completed for each identified PMEF candidate.

Table 6: PMEF Candidate Worksheet Column Descriptions

WORKSHEET COLUMN	DESCRIPTION
PMEF Entry #	Enter the sequential number of the identified PMEF Candidate
Dept/Agency	Enter department or agency identification
Sub-element or Department component	Identify subordinate elements, if applicable
Primary Mission Essential Function Statement (Candidate statement based on organizational mission and relates to identified MEFs linked to the NEFs from proceeding worksheet)	Identify the PMEF candidate. This column should include those functions that embody the specificity of the organizational mission and consist of one or more MEFs that are linked to NEF execution.
NEF 1. Ensuring the continued functioning of our form of government under the Constitution, including the functioning of the three separate branches of government.	Place the letter 'X' in the cell if this PMEF candidate supports this NEF. There can be more than one NEF selected for each PMEF candidate.
NEF 2. Providing leadership visible to the Nation and the world and maintaining the trust and confidence of the American people.	Place the letter 'X' in the cell if this PMEF candidate supports this NEF. There can be more than one NEF selected for each PMEF candidate.
NEF 3. Defending the Constitution of the United States against all enemies, foreign and domestic, and preventing or interdicting attacks against the United States or its people, property, or interests.	Place the letter 'X' in the cell if this PMEF candidate supports this NEF. There can be more than one NEF selected for each PMEF candidate.
NEF 4. Maintaining and fostering effective relationships with foreign nations.	Place the letter 'X' in the cell if this PMEF candidate supports this NEF. There can be more than one NEF selected for each PMEF candidate.
NEF 5. Protecting against threats to the homeland and bringing to justice perpetrators of crimes or attacks against the United States or its people, property, or interests.	Place the letter 'X' in the cell if this PMEF candidate supports this NEF. There can be more than one NEF selected for each PMEF candidate.
NEF 6. Providing rapid and effective response to and recovery from the domestic consequences of an attack or other incident.	Place the letter 'X' in the cell if this PMEF candidate supports this NEF. There can be more than one NEF selected for each PMEF candidate.
NEF 7. Protecting and stabilizing the Nation's economy and ensuring public confidence in its financial systems.	Place the letter 'X' in the cell if this PMEF candidate supports this NEF. There can be more than one NEF selected for each PMEF candidate.
NEF 8. Providing for critical Federal Government services that address the national health, safety, and welfare needs of the United States.	Place the letter 'X' in the cell if this PMEF candidate supports this NEF. There can be more than one NEF selected for each PMEF candidate.
Associated MEF Entry Numbers	Enter the MEF Entry Number from the previous worksheets that are associated to the PMEF candidate.
ID D/A action or role	Place an 'X' in the cell if the PMEF statement clearly identifies the department's or agency's action or role in completing the PMEF candidate.
ID conditions for PMEF	Place an 'X' in the cell if the PMEF statement clearly identifies the department's or agency's conditions under which the PMEF candidate would be performed.
ID scope of operations	Place an 'X' in the cell if the PMEF statement clearly identifies the department's or agency's scope of operations.
PMEF standard of performance	Place an 'X' in the cell if the PMEF statement clearly identifies the department's or agency's PMEF standard of performance.
Maximum Tolerable Downtime	Enter the maximum number of hours for which it is acceptable that the PMEF candidate can be interrupted following a continuity event.

WORKSHEET COLUMN	DESCRIPTION
List internal and external partners required to perform function	List, by name, the organization(s) required to perform this PMEF.
D/A CC Validated	The department or agency Continuity Coordinator initials that the PMEF candidate can support a NEF. Any PMEF candidate that is not required within 12 hours of interruption will require further explanation in the narrative submission of the process.

The candidate PMEFs for consideration are entered on the PMEF Business Impact Analysis (BIA) Worksheet pending IAB review of submitted potential PMEFs, which will validate their relationship to the NEFs. Those MEFs that meet the PMEF screening criteria should be submitted with a Candidate PMEF Narrative Sheet, which will provide insight into the BIA that ensures the PMEFs are appropriate and relevant.

Candidate PMEF Narrative Sheet

In support of the Potential PMEF Submission Workbook, agencies will also prepare Candidate PMEF Narrative Sheets. These sheets will include organization and point of contact; PMEF statement; PMEF description; implications if the PMEF is not performed; supporting MEF(s) linked to each PMEF; supported NEFs; maximum tolerable downtime; and interdependent partnerships. The Candidate PMEF Narrative Sheet is provided as Attachment D.

POTENTIAL PMEF SUBMISSION

As mandated by the National Continuity Policy Implementation Plan, agencies' potential PMEFs and supporting materials must be submitted to DHS within 90 days of receiving DHS' submission guidance. The submission package includes a memorandum from the agency head, confirming the validation of the agency's MEFs and PMEFs and identifying the potential PMEFs for submission and review by the IAB. This memorandum should also include the contact information (name, email address, and phone number) for the department's or agency's Continuity Coordinator and Continuity Manager for potential follow-up coordination. Additional elements to be included in the Potential PMEF Submission Package include the completed MS Excel workbook (with the exception of the PMEF BIA Worksheet) for each MEF that the department or agency nominates as a potential PMEF.

PMEF BUSINESS IMPACT ANALYSIS (BIA)

Agencies will complete a BIA once they have received the approved PMEFs. This will be completed after the IAB and the agency has completed a joint review and validation of the potential PMEFs and the NCC has approved the PMEFs. Each agency BIA will be completed by using the worksheet described below. As agencies are identifying threats and potential vulnerabilities associated with the PMEFs in the BIA process, they should coordinate with their security managers to ensure the information included in the BIA has the appropriate level of classification.

PMEF Business Impact Analysis (BIA) Worksheet

The PMEF BIA Worksheet (see Figure 16) is provided to assist agencies in conducting the BIAs on each of their PMEFs, identifying threats or hazards and their possible impact on each potential PMEF and their associated NEF. The worksheet takes into consideration the impact, potential downtime, and mandated recovery times, and provides a stoplight analysis (red, yellow, green) of the potential impact for developing mitigation strategies. Once the analysis is completed, the department or agency Continuity Coordinator reviews and validates the BIA by initialing the worksheet in the column, as indicated.

Figure 16: PMEF BIA Worksheet

Table 7 shows the component details for the PMEF BIA Worksheet. Each column in the worksheet is described below to assist the user in completing the worksheet. For this worksheet, a separate row should be completed for each identified threat or hazard associated with a particular PMEF.

Table 7: PMEF BIA Worksheet Column Descriptions

WORKSHEET COLUMN	DESCRIPTION
Entry #	Enter the sequential number of the identified PMEF
Dept/Agency	Enter department or agency identification
Sub-element or Department component	Identify subordinate element, if applicable
Primary Mission Essential Function	Identify the PMEF candidate. This column should include those MEFs that met the PMEF screening requirements. Does not include enabling or supporting tasks. Does not include capability requirements.
Identify Threat or Hazard	Identify the potential threat or hazard to be considered when determining the impact on PMEF support to the NEF(s).
Vulnerability - Identify potential point of failure	Comment on the vulnerability and potential point of failure of the PMEF to the identified threat or hazard.
Vulnerability Value	Determine the vulnerability value for a PMEF in the event of the identified crisis/hazard situation or emergency. Consider the criticality of the outputs/products that would result from the completion of the function. Vulnerability is assessed 1-10 using a drop-down menu on the spreadsheet.

<table>
<tr><td>

- **10-Critically High** Exceptionally grave vulnerability to mission performance and the ability to implement corrective actions
- **9-Extremely High** Grave vulnerability, where negative effect results in delays to mission for an extended period of time
- **8-Very High** Serious vulnerability, where negative effect results in delays to mission for a limited period of time
- **7-High** Serious vulnerability, where the negative effect results in minor mission delays
- **6-Medium High** Moderate to

</td><td>

- **5-Medium** Moderate vulnerability, where the negative effect results in no impact to mission completion
- **4-Medium Low** Minimal vulnerability, where negative effect results in no impact to mission completion
- **3-Low** Minimal vulnerability of consequence without long term negative effects
- **2-Very Low** Negligible vulnerability of consequences with minimal long term negative effect
- **1-Extremely Low** Negligible vulnerability of consequences with no long term negative effect

</td></tr>
</table>

WORKSHEET COLUMN	DESCRIPTION
	serious vulnerability, where the negative effect results in slight mission delays
Assess Event Likelihood	Comment on the likelihood of the identified threat or hazard occurring.
Likelihood Value	Determine the Likelihood of the identified crisis/hazard situation or emergency. Likelihood is assessed 1-10 using a drop-down menu on the spreadsheet with 1 being very unlikely and 10 being very likely to occur. • **10-Critically High** • **5-Medium** • **9-Extremely High** • **4-Medium Low** • **8-Very High** • **3-Low** • **7-High** • **2-Very Low** • **6-Medium High** • **1-Extremely Low**
Impact of PMEF failure or downtime on supported NEF(s)	Comment on the impact to the PMEF by the identified threat or hazard.
Impact Value	Determine the Impact of the failure of the identified PMEF in the event of the identified crisis/hazard situation or emergency. Consider the criticality of the outputs/products that would result from the completion of the function. Vulnerability is assessed 1-10 using a drop-down menu on the spreadsheet: • **10-Critically High** Exceptionally grave impact preventing mission performance and the ability to implement corrective actions • **9-Extremely High** Grave impact requiring corrective action and negative effect results in delays to mission for an extended period of time • **8-Very High** Serious impact requiring corrective action and negative effect results in delays to mission for a limited period of time • **7-High** Serious impact requiring corrective action, where the negative effect results in minor mission delays • **6-Medium High** Moderate to serious impact requiring corrective action, where the negative effect results in slight mission delays • **5-Medium** Moderate impact requiring corrective action, where the negative effect results in no impact to mission completion • **4-Medium Low** Minimal impact requiring corrective action, where negative effect results in no impact to mission completion • **3-Low** Minimal impact or consequence without long term negative effects • **2-Very Low** Negligible consequences or impact with minimal long term negative effect • **1-Extremely Low** Negligible consequences or impact with no long term negative effect
Potential Downtime	Estimate the potential downtime as a result of the identified threat or hazard.
Mandated Recovery Time	Define the mandated recovery time for the PMEF support to the NEF(s).
Risk Assessment Value	The risk assessment value is the sum of the Vulnerability, the Likelihood, and the Impact of the Threat or Hazard on a PMEF support to the NEF(s). The value is automatically summed in the worksheet.
Impact Analysis: Red-High Yellow-Med Green-Low	Determine the impact of PMEF downtime and/or failure on the execution of the NEF(s) • **Red-High (21-30)** Based on the risk, vulnerability and impact on the NEF for PMEF failure is high. • **Yellow-Moderate (11-20)** Based on the risk, vulnerability and impact on the NEF for PMEF failure is moderate. • **Green-Low (1-10)** Based on the risk, vulnerability and impact on the NEF for PMEF failure is low.

WORKSHEET COLUMN	DESCRIPTION
Mitigation Strategy (include policy, geographical dispersion, redundant capabilities, etc)	Identify, create, and formalize PMEF process alternatives / work-around to execute NEF(s). Identify the risk mitigation strategy that is planned by the department or agency.
D/A CC Validated	The department or agency Continuity Coordinator initials that an impact analysis has been conducted and risk mitigation strategies have been developed for all hazards/threats to PMEF candidates support to a NEF(s).
IAB Validation	IAB reports to the NCC with their findings and recommendations related to the PMEF process.

CONCLUSION

This formalized process for identification and submission of a department's or agency's MEFs and potential PMEFs that are consistent and supportive of the NEFs is critical to maintaining an effective national continuity capability. All department or agencies are required to submit a package even if they do not have any candidate PMEFs. These submissions will then be reviewed by the IAB for PMEF identification and approval as outlined in Annex A, Appendix 1. By following the processes outlined in this FCD, departments and agencies support the continuation of the NEFs through the identification of those supporting PMEFs, thus ensuring the preservation of our form of government under the Constitution for all of our Nation's citizens.

ANNEX A – APPENDIX 1
PROCESS FOR PMEF IDENTIFICATION

PMEF identification is an iterative process performed by each department and agency in coordination with the NCC. In order to identify and analyze PMEFs, the following actions will take place as part of the IAB process for PMEF identification. (see Figure 17):

- Upon MEF approval by each department or agency head, a joint effort between the NCC and each department or agency Continuity Coordinator and staff will result in a preliminary identification of PMEFs that potentially support NEFs. The joint effort will culminate in the department or agency's submission of PMEF identification results to the NCC for further interagency analysis.

- An IAB, established by the NCC, conducts a review of submitted potential PMEFs and validates PMEFs' relationship to the NEFs. A risk management methodology (i.e., BIA) will be used to ensure that the PMEFs'are appropriate and relevant.

- Upon confirmation that the IAB has determined that a department or agency's MEF shall serve as a PMEF, each department and agency will revisit the prioritization of their MEF recovery timelines to ensure PMEF criticality.

- The IAB will conduct a BPA to identify and map interagency PMEF processes, workflows, activities, expertise, systems, data, and facilities inherent to the interagency execution of each NEF. The BPA should also define the PMEF relationship to the NEF. In other words, the BPA will define how each NEF is executed via business process flow mapping (i.e., NEF serving as the "end product output" and interagency PMEF serving as the functional "inputs").

- The IAB must also conduct an analysis of interagency PMEF interdependencies within each NEF to accurately depict each department or agency's PMEF execution capability and dependencies. The IAB will conduct NEF-specific BIAs to: (1) identify potential single points of failure that may adversely affect the execution of the interagency PMEF support to NEFs; (2) define the impact of downtime (i.e., impact of delayed PMEF recovery on NEF execution); and (3) define potential PMEF process alternatives/work-around solutions.

- The NEF BPAs, BIAs, and the interagency list of PMEFs are submitted to the NCC for final approval.

Interagency Board (IAB) PMEF Business Process Analysis (BPA)
IAB conducts a BPA to identify and map interagency PMEF processes, workflows, activities, expertise, systems, data, and facilities inherent to the interagency execution of the NEF.

IAB PMEF Interdependencies Analysis
IAB conducts further detailed PMEF BPA to identify and map interagency PMEF interdependencies required to execute support to the NEF.

IAB NEF-specific Business Impact Analysis (BIA)
IAB conducts a detailed NEF BIA to:
1) Identify interagency potential single points of failure which may adversely affect the execution of the NEF;
2) Define the impact of PMEF downtime and/or failure on the execution of the NEF(s);
3) Define mandated timelines for recovery for PMEF support to each NEF; and
4) Identify, create, and formalize PMEF process alternatives/workarounds to execute NEFs.

IAB Submits NEF BPA & BIA Reports to the NCC
IAB compiles and submits final NEF BPA Mapping and BIA Report with findings and recommendations for mitigation, risk reduction, and risk management actions for each NEF. Risk management options shall include policy development, business process reengineering, asset dispersion, continuity system(s) design redundancy and survivability requirements, and other relevant options.

NCC Reviews BPA/BIA Findings to:
1) Identify continuity program shortcomings;
2) Determine program shortcomings to initiate policy revision and development efforts;
3) Define future continuity program requirements and standards of performance;
4) Relate continuity program budget and funding requirements to risk management; and
5) Manage and lead the Federal Government continuity program efforts as the NCC.

Figure 17: Process for PMEF Identification

ANNEX B. GLOSSARY

Business Impact Analysis – A method of identifying the effects of failing to perform a function or requirement.

Business Process Analysis – A method of examining, identifying, and mapping the functional processes, workflows, activities, personnel expertise, systems, data, and facilities inherent to the execution of a function or requirement.

Government Functions – Government functions include both the collective functions of the heads of agencies as defined by statute, regulations, presidential direction, or other legal authority, and the functions of the legislative and judicial branches.

Interagency Board – A working group established by the NCC to review and recommend validation of potential PMEFs submitted by agencies for submission to the NCC for final approval.

Mandated Recovery Time: The legally or organizationally specified time objective that identifies the allowable time from interruption until system/function recovery.

Maximum Tolerable Downtime (MTD): The maximum number of hours for which it is acceptable that a function can be interrupted following a continuity event.

Mission Essential Functions (MEFs): The limited set of agency-level government functions that must be continued after a disruption of normal activities

National Essential Functions (NEFs): The eight functions the President and national leadership will focus on to lead and sustain the nation during a catastrophic emergency.

Potential PMEF Submission Package: This includes the Agency Memorandum from the agency head, confirming the validation of the agency's MEFs and PMEFs and identifying the potential PMEFs for submission and review by the Interagency Board (IAB); and the MEF/PMEF Workbook which is a compilation of worksheets, located in Attachment A, which identify requirements, inputs, outputs, interdependencies and other critical elements that assist agencies in identifying their MEFs and potential PMEFs and completing the required BPAs.

Primary Mission Essential Functions (PMEFs): Those department and agency Mission Essential Functions, validated by the NCC, which must be performed in order to support the performance of NEFs before, during, and in the aftermath of an emergency. PMEFs need to be continuous or resumed within 12 hours after an event and maintained for up to 30 days or until normal operations can be resumed.

Risk Management: The process of identifying, controlling, and minimizing the impact of events whose consequences are or may be unknown, or events that are themselves fraught with uncertainty.

ANNEX C. AUTHORITIES AND REFERENCES

The following are the authorities and references for this FCD.

AUTHORITIES:

1) The National Security Act of 1947 (50 U.S.C. § 404), July 26, 1947.

2) Homeland Security Act of 2002 (6 U.S.C. § 101 *et seq.*), November 25, 2002.

3) Executive Order 12148, *Federal Emergency Management*, July 20, 1979, as amended.

4) Executive Order 12472, *Assignment of National Security and Emergency Preparedness Telecommunications Functions*, April 3, 1984, as amended.

5) Executive Order 12656, *Assignment of Emergency Preparedness Responsibilities*, November 18, 1988, as amended.

6) Executive Order 13286, *Establishing the Office of Homeland Security*, February 28, 2003.

7) National Security Presidential Directive 51/Homeland Security Presidential Directive 20, *National Continuity Policy*, May 9, 2007.

8) Homeland Security Presidential Directive 7, *Critical Infrastructure Identification, Prioritization, and Protection*, December 17, 2003.

9) Homeland Security Presidential Directive 8, *National Preparedness*, December 17, 2003.

10) National Continuity Policy Implementation Plan, August 2007.

11) National Communications System Directive 3-10, *Minimum Requirements for Continuity Communications Capabilities*, July 25, 2007.

REFERENCES:

1) 36 C.F.R., Part 1236, *Management of Vital Records*.

2) 41 C.F.R. 101.20.103-4, *Occupant Emergency Program*.

3) Presidential Decision Directive 62, *Protection Against Unconventional Threats to the Homeland and Americans Overseas*, May 22, 1998.

4) Homeland Security Presidential Directive 1, *Organization and Operation of the Homeland Security Council*, October 29, 2001.

5) Homeland Security Presidential Directive 3, *Homeland Security Advisory System*, March 11, 2002.

6) Homeland Security Presidential Directive 5, *Management of Domestic Incidents*, February 28, 2003.

7) Homeland Security Presidential Directive 12, *Policy for a Common Identification Standard for Federal Employees and Contractors*, August 27, 2004.

8) Federal Continuity Directive 1 (FCD 1), January 2008.

9) National Infrastructure Protection Plan, January 2006.

10) National Strategy for Pandemic Influenza, November 1, 2005.

11) National Strategy for Pandemic Influenza Implementation Plan, May 2006.

12) National Exercise Program Implementation Plan, April 2007.

13) National Incident Management System (NIMS), March 1, 2004.

14) NIST Special Publication 800-34, *Contingency Planning Guide for Information Technology Systems,* June 2002.

15) NIST Special Publication 800-53, *Recommended Security Controls for Federal Information Systems,* December 2006.

16) NFPA 1600 Standard on Disaster/Emergency Management and Business Continuity Programs, 2007 Edition.